MW01706768

Proofreading

Capitalization, Punctuation & Spelling

Grade 3

Written by
Kathleen Knoblock

Illustrated by
Mark Mason

Published by **Frank Schaffer Publications, Inc.**
23740 Hawthorne Blvd.
Torrance, CA 90505

Name ______________________________

Our Field Trip

In the story below, these important rules for using capital letters were forgotten. Read the story and underline the 17 letters that should be capitals.

Rule: Capitalize the first word of a sentence.
Examples: The wind was strong. **I** heard the door slam. **T**hen I ran.

Rule: Capitalize the first, last, and all important words in a title.
Examples: I saw "**T**he **W**izard of **O**z." My project is "**S**hells of the **S**ea."

our field trip

on Thursday our class took a field trip to the Air and Space Museum. in a large theater we saw the movie "to fly." the movie told about the history of flying from the first airplane through space travel.

next we saw the exhibits. i liked the ones called "what it's like on the moon" and "those flying machines." I think our field trip was terrific!

Rewrite the story correctly on the lines below.

____

____

____

____

____

____

____

____

____

____

____

____

Brainwork! Write a story about a field trip you would like to take. Include names of things to see and do there.

Name ______________________________

Summer Vacation

In the story below, these important rules for using capital letters were forgotten. Read the story and underline the 11 letters that should be capitals.

Rule: Capitalize the names of particular places.
Example: We went to **S**ea **W**orld in **S**an **D**iego, **C**alifornia.

Rule: Capitalize the names of days, months, and holidays.
Example: My birthday is on **F**riday, **M**ay 31, which is **M**emorial **D**ay.

Summer Vacation

Every august Jimmy and Jenny take a trip with their family. This year Jenny wanted to go to disney World in orlando, florida. Jimmy wanted to visit his friend who had moved last thanksgiving to savannah, georgia. Dad solved the twins' problem. "First we'll stop in savannah and spend sunday with Jimmy's friend. Next we'll drive down the coast and be in Orlando on wednesday. Then we'll spend the rest of our vacation at Disney world."

Rewrite the story correctly on the lines below.

Brainwork! Write what your dream vacation would be like. When would you take it? Where would you go?

The New Principal

In the story below, these important rules for using capital letters were forgotten. Read the story and underline the 13 letters that should be capitals.

Rule: Any person's name or any title that is part of the name begins with a capital letter.
Example: **M**r. **D**avis took his daughter **L**iz to see **D**r. **F**rancis **G**ould.

Rule: Any time you use *I* in place of your name it is capitalized.
Example: **I** was invited, but **I** couldn't go because **I** was sick.

The New Principal

The students were at an assembly. Our retiring principal, mr. hunt, had asked us to gather to meet his replacement. "I'd like you to meet dr. barbara newley," he said.

As the new principal walked in, my teacher mrs. lowe, leaned over and whispered to me, "carmen, please ask miss compton for the roses we got for the new principal. Then present them to dr. newley." Of all the students , i had been chosen to welcome the new principal!

Rewrite the story correctly on the lines below.

Brainwork! Write a paragraph that tells how each of these people might have felt during the assembly: Mr. Hunt, Dr. Newley, Carmen.

Name ________________________ Skill: Proofreading, Capitalization review

Man of Peace

In the story below, these important rules for using capital letters were forgotten. Read the story and underline the 13 letters that should be capitals.

Rule: A person's name or title that is part of the name begins with a capital letter.
Example: **D**r. **N**orris saw **M**rs. **D**avies first, then **F**rank **L**ee, **J**r.

Rule: Capitalize the first word of a sentence.
Examples: **T**oday is warm. **I** like warm days. **Y**esterday was warm, too.

Rule: Capitalize the names of particular places.
Example: She was born in **A**lbany, **N**ew **Y**ork.

Man of Peace

americans remember martin luther king, jr. as a man of peace. growing up in atlanta, georgia, martin noticed that sometimes people were treated differently only because of the color of their skin. believing in equality for all people, dr. king devoted his life to showing others how to change unjust laws in nonviolent ways. though Dr. King is now gone, his dream of equality lives on.

Rewrite the story correctly on the lines below.

Brainwork! In 1964, Dr. King was awarded a special prize. Find out what it was, and where and why it was given to him. Write your findings.

Name ______________________ Skill: Proofreading, Capitalization review

Special Days

In the story below, these important rules for using capital letters were forgotten. Read the story and underline the 20 letters that should be capitals.

Rule: Any time you use *I* in place of your name, it is capitalized.
Example: The holiday **I** like best is Thanksgiving.

Rule: Capitalize the first, last, and all important words in a title.
Example: The stories were called "**B**eing **M**y **F**riend" and "**I**n the **S**un."

Rule: Capitalize the names of days, months, and holidays.
Example: This **S**unday, **J**une 21, is **F**ather's **D**ay.

Special days

I have favorite special days of the year. I like valentine's day because it brightens up february. In may, i enjoy making Mom things for mother's day like my book of poems called "collecting my thoughts." My birthday makes august special. Another favorite of mine is halloween, especially if october 31 falls on a friday or saturday. Maybe best of all is new year's day because i know another whole year of special days is on its way.

Rewrite the story correctly on the lines below.

Brainwork! Write a story that tells about your three favorite special days of the year. Include a title and remember the capitalization rules.

Name ______________________________ Skill: Proofreading, Punctuation

Windy Weather

In the story below, these important rules for using punctuation were forgotten. Read the story and add 12 periods, two question marks, and one exclamation point.

Rule: A sentence ends with a period (.), question mark (?), or exclamation point (!).
Examples: I like windy weather. Do you**?** I think it's great**!**

Rule: Place periods where words have been shortened in abbreviations.
Examples: The driver went 20 **m.p.h**. down Darrel **Ave.**

Windy Weather

Once when I was two years old, the wind blew me over. How could something I couldn't see knock me down

Wind is simply moving air Sometimes the air seems almost still Other times the wind is so strong it can push over a big tree The force of the wind is measured in miles per hour (m p h). At four to seven m p h you may feel a slight breeze. At 32 m p h it's hard to walk against the wind What do you think the speed of the wind was when it blew me over

Rewrite the story correctly on the lines below.

____

____

____

____

____

____

____

____

____

____

____

____

____

Brainwork! Tornados, hurricanes, and blizzards are types of storms that combine strong winds with rain or snow. Find out and write about one of these types of storms.

Dinosaur Days

In the story below, these two important rules for using commas were forgotten. Read the story and put in the nine missing commas.

Rule: In a sentence, use commas after items in a list.
Example: I like apples, oranges, peaches, and pears.

Rule: Use commas between two or more words that describe one thing.
Example: The queen wore a sparkling, glittering, jeweled crown.

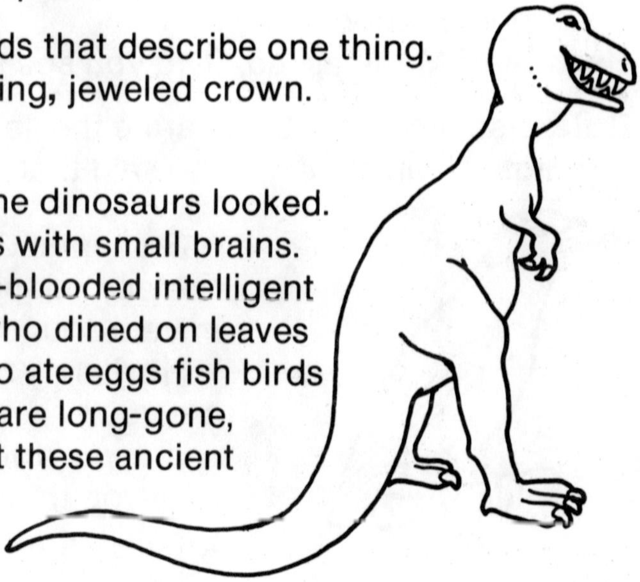

Dinosaur Days

Scientists have different ideas about how the dinosaurs looked. Some think they were big green scaly reptiles with small brains. Others think that some dinosaurs were warm-blooded intelligent animals. Some dinosaurs were plant-eaters who dined on leaves grass and fruits. Others were meat-eaters who ate eggs fish birds and other dinosaurs. Even though dinosaurs are long-gone, scientists keep making new discoveries about these ancient fascinating creatures.

Rewrite the story correctly on the lines below.

Brainwork! Begin a sentence with *I like...* and list your favorite foods. Do the same for your favorite games and things to do. Use commas in your lists.

Name ______________________________

My Myna Dinah

In the story below, these important rules about quotations were forgotten. Read the story and put in two commas and three sets of quotation marks.

Rule: To quote exact words said, place opening quotation marks before the first spoken word. Place closing quotation marks after the last spoken word and punctuation.

Examples: Marie asked, "Did you see that?"; "What a hit!" said Don.

Rule: Use a comma to separate the speaker's words from the rest of the sentence.

Example: Jean asked, "Who said that?"

My Myna Dinah

Someone came to my door. My myna Dinah said Hello!

Many people think myna birds can talk, but they only imitate sounds.

How are you? asked the visitor, and Dinah replied How are you?

A myna's voice sounds surprisingly human. So the next time you think someone is talking to you, it could be Dinah—or some other myna!

Rewrite the story correctly on the lines below.

Brainwork! Write a conversation you might have with a myna like Dinah. Use quotation marks.

Name ______________________________ Skill: Proofreading, Punctuation review

News Flash!

In the news story below, these important rules for using commas in dates and periods in abbreviations were forgotten. Read the story and put in three commas and seven periods.

Rule: When writing a date, place a comma between the day and the year.
Example: The meeting was held on May 2, 1987.

Rule: Place periods where words have been shortened in abbreviations.
Example: On **Oct.** 12, **Mrs. B.** Hatcher of Layton **St.** will begin a tour of the **U.S.A.**

News Flash!

On Nov 30 1987, the city spelling bee finally ended. Lee Hahn of 1412 Lyon Ave accepted his first-place prize of one hundred dollars on Dec 1 1987. A ceremony was held at City Hall hosted by Mr Alex Bate, U S senator from Missouri. Lee was one of eighty students who entered the contest on Sept 9 1987. His winning word was "leprechaun."

Rewrite the story correctly on the lines below.

Brainwork! Imagine that you were honored in a ceremony. Write a news story about the event including where, when, and why you were honored.

Name ______________________________ Skill: Proofreading, Punctuation review

Night Visitor

In the story below, these important rules for using commas and quotation marks were forgotten. Read the story and put in eight missing commas and four sets of missing quotation marks.

Rule: Use commas between a list of two or more words that describe one thing.
Example: My bike was old, rusty, and broken.

Rule: To quote exact words said, place opening quotation marks before the first spoken word. Place closing quotation marks after the last spoken word and punctuation.
Examples: Kyle asked, "Did you see it?" "I did!" shouted Ned.

Night Visitor

It was a quiet peaceful night. Suddenly I heard a whirring sound outside my window. I looked out to see that a spaceship had landed! It was silver red gold and green. The door opened. Out walked an alien whose hair was fuzzy purple and strange. It had a round red and cute nose. Is this the planet Zick? he asked.

No. I said.

Sorry, he replied, wrong planet. The door closed and the ship left as suddenly as it had come.

Brainwork! Write your own story about an imaginary encounter with an alien. What would you say to each other? Use quotation marks around any spoken parts.

Name ______________________________ Skill: Proofreading, Spelling

Chester's Fur Flaps

In the story below, some words sound right, but have the wrong spelling for their meaning. They are homonyms. Look at these sets of homonyms and their meanings. Read the story and circle the seven homonyms that are incorrect.

Set 1:	**their**—belongs to them	**they're**—they are	**there**—a place
Examples:	I saw **their** new car.	**They're** leaving.	Let's go **there**.
Set 2:	**to**—movement toward	**too**—extreme, also	**two**—number 2
Examples:	Go **to** the store.	I'm **too** hot, **too**!	I ate **two** pieces.

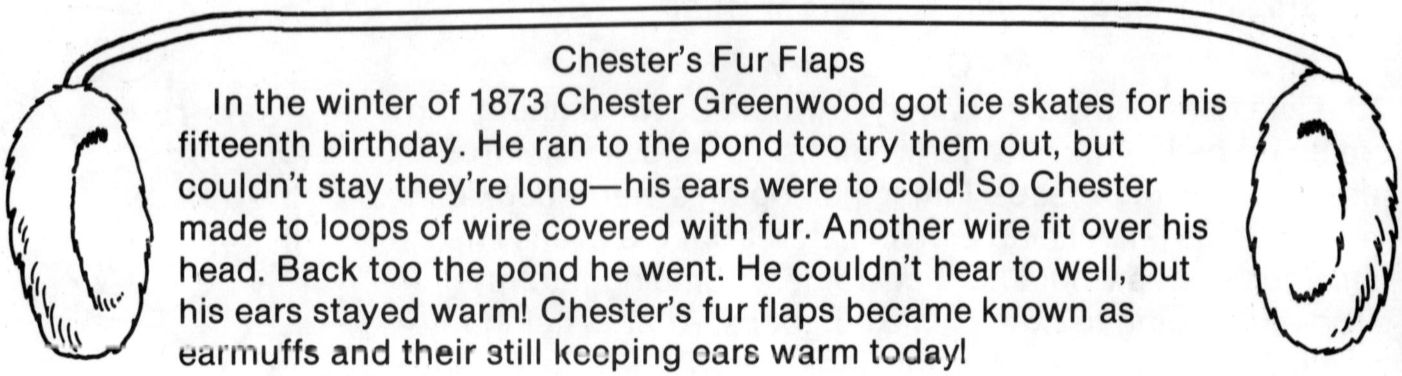

Chester's Fur Flaps

In the winter of 1873 Chester Greenwood got ice skates for his fifteenth birthday. He ran to the pond too try them out, but couldn't stay they're long—his ears were to cold! So Chester made to loops of wire covered with fur. Another wire fit over his head. Back too the pond he went. He couldn't hear to well, but his ears stayed warm! Chester's fur flaps became known as earmuffs and their still keeping ears warm today!

Rewrite the story correctly on the lines below.

____

____

____

____

____

____

____

____

____

____

____

____

____

Brainwork! Chester invented earmuffs because he needed something that hadn't been invented. Describe something you need that hasn't yet been invented.

Name ____________________ Skill: Proofreading, Spelling

My Own Bakery

In the story below, these important spelling guidelines have been forgotten. Read the story and circle the 11 misspelled words.

Guideline 1: If a word ends with a single vowel and a single consonant, double the last letter before adding an ending.

Examples: h**op**-ho**pp***ing* sw**im**-sw**imm***ing* beg**in**-beg**inn***ing*

Guideline 2: If a word ends with silent *e*, the *e* is dropped before adding an ending.

Examples: hop**e**-hop*ing* wast**e**-wast*ing* decid**e**-decid*ing*

My Own Bakery

I'd like to have my own bakery. It would be fun planing and createing beautiful cakes for wedings. I'd enjoy makeing pies and bakeing breads. I imagine poping a warm cookie in my mouth as I'm takeing a fresh batch from the oven. The delicious scents would have customers comeing into my shop and beging to buy my baked goods. After tasteing my creations, they'd surely be smileing!

Rewrite the story correctly on the lines below.

Brainwork! What job or career do you imagine having when you grow up? What kinds of things would you do in your job? Write about it.

Name ______________________________

My Dream

In the poem below, these important spelling guidelines for making words plural were forgotten. Read the poem. Circle the seven misspelled words.

Guideline 1: If a word ends with *f* or *fe,* change the *f* to *v* and add *es* to make it plural.
Examples: half-halves leaf-leaves knife-knives

Guideline 2: If a word ends with *s*, *x*, *sh*, or *ch* add *es* to make it plural.
Examples: kiss-kisses tax-taxes dish-dishes ranch-ranches

Guideline 3: If a word ends with a *y* that sounds like *ee*, change the *y* to *i* and add *es* to make it plural.
Examples: party-parties penny-pennies lady-ladies

My Dream

Last night I dreamed I joined the elfs
Who make the toys on toy-shop shelfs.
We made the toys to fill wishs and hopes,
From stuffed little puppys to long jump ropes,
From dolls with brushs to comb their fine hair,
To rattles for babys and skates by the pair.
What fun with the elfs I had last night,
'Til I woke up this morning and found it was light.

Rewrite the poem correctly on the lines below. Begin each line with a capital letter.

____

____

____

____

____

____

____

____

____

____

Brainwork! List ten of your wishes. Trade lists with a friend. Read the lists and find any misspelled words.

Name ______________________________ Skill: Proofreading, Spelling

Best Friends

In the story below are some commonly misspelled words. Use these guidelines to help you recognize them. Then read the story. Circle the six misspelled words.

Guideline 1: Look for letters that are out of order in a word.

Examples: bec**au**se not bec**ua**se
fr**ie**nd not fr**ei**nd
p**ie**ce not p**ei**ce

Guideline 2: Look for missing letters in a word.

Examples: Feb**r**uary not Febuary
We**d**nesday not Wenesday
lib**r**ary not libary

Best Friends

Today is not just any Wednesday—it's a special Wenesday. A year ago today, Febuary 18, I met my best friend Katie. While I was in the libary, it started to snow. I didn't notice becuase I was busy reading. Later, Katie and I just happened to leave the library at the same time. We ended up walking home together in the snow. We exchanged phone numbers on a torn peice of paper. That snowy day was the beginning of our freindship.

Rewrite the story correctly on the lines below.

____

____

____

____

____

____

____

____

____

____

____

____

____

Brainwork! Write a story about your best friend. Tell how you met and became friends. When you are finished, proofread your story.

Name ______________________________

Moving Day

In the story below, these important rules of capitalization, punctuation, and spelling were forgotten. Read the story and underline the seven letters that should be capitals, put in the five missing commas, and circle the five misspelled words.

Rule: Names of particular places should begin with a capital letter.
Example: My cousin in **P**hoenix, **A**rizona lives on **C**amelback **R**oad.

Rule: In a sentence, use commas after items in a list.
Example: Bill took a tent**,** sleeping bag**,** backpack**,** and flashlight.

Rule: Usually if a word ends with silent *e*, the *e* is dropped before adding an ending.
Examples: Are you **coming** along? (com**e**) I was **making** dinner. (mak**e**)

Moving Day

It was moveing day for Pete and his family. Mom was takeing a terrific new job in richmond, virginia. She told Pete that presidents Washington Jefferson and Madison were born there and that Pete would even be liveing on monroe street! Pete packed his cap mitt baseball and team shirt. He'd miss his friends in grove city, california, but looked forward to makeing new friends and haveing new kinds of fun!

Rewrite the story correctly on the lines below.

____

____

____

____

____

____

____

____

____

____

____

____

Brainwork! Write the ways in which Pete's life might be the same and different in Virginia and California.

Dear Mr. Sobol

In the letter below, these important rules for writing a friendly letter were forgotten. Read the letter. Underline the three letters that should be capitals and put in the three missing commas.

Rule: When writing a date, capitalize the first letter of the month and place a comma between the day and year.

Example: **A**pril 21**,** 1987

Rule: In the greeting of a letter, capitalize the word *Dear* and place a comma after the name of the person being addressed.

Example: **D**ear Encyclopedia Brown**,**

Rule: In the closing of a letter, capitalize the first word and place a comma after the last word.

Example: **Y**our friend**,**

january 30 1988

dear Mr. Donald Sobol

I really enjoy reading your Encyclopedia Brown books. Each adventure is fresh and the clues keep me on my toes. How do you ever think of all those different mysteries to solve? I think they are all terrific. What a great way to spend an afternoon—with that super sleuth—Encyclopedia Brown!

your fan
Chris

Rewrite the letter correctly on the lines below.

____

____

____

____

____

____

____

____

____

____

____

Brainwork! Write a letter to an author whose books you really enjoy. Use correct letter form.

Name ______________________________ Skill: Proofreading, Letter form

It's Our Birthday!

In the letter below, a few important rules for writing a letter were forgotten. Read the letter. Underline the nine letters that should be capitals, put in seven missing commas, and add two periods, three question marks, and one exclamation point.

june 27 1990

dear josé

Did you know that I was born on july 4 1976 That was America's 200th birthday

Can you help us celebrate our birthday by coming to my party next saturday at 6:00 Dan jill Mark and tommy are invited, too We'll have a cookout and play games Then we'll all go to see fireworks. Will you let me know if you'll be there

your friend
glen

Rewrite the letter correctly on the lines below.

Brainwork! With whom would you like to share a birth date? How would you celebrate your birthday together? Write a letter inviting this person to your special birthday celebration. Use correct letter form.

Name ______________________ Skill: Proofreading, Capitalization

Jane and the Chimps

In the story below, rules for using capital letters for names of particular people and places, to begin a sentence, and in titles were forgotten. Read the story and underline the 17 letters that should be capitals.

jane and the chimps

jane goodall is a famous zoologist—a scientist who studies animals. born in london, england, jane went to africa to live among the chimpanzees and study their behavior. she discovered that chimps share many behaviors with humans.

jane observed that chimps eat meat, not just plants. they also teach their young, fight among themselves, and use twigs and stems as tools to help dig for termites in holes. jane told about her important discoveries in writings such as "my friends, the wild chimpanzees."

Rewrite the story correctly on the lines below.

Brainwork! Imagine that you are a zoologist. What animal would you study? Where would you go to study it? What might you find out about it? Write about your imaginary study. Proofread your work for capitals.

Name ______________________ Skill: Proofreading, Punctuation

Americans in Space

In the story below, important rules for using periods, commas, and quotation marks were forgotten. Read the story and put in the missing punctuation marks. (Hint: Four abbreviations and three sentences are missing periods. Three commas are missing—two in dates and one before a quotation. One set of quotation marks is missing.)

Americans in Space

On Feb 20 1962, John Glenn, Jr became the first American to orbit the earth. His flight lasted 4 hrs 56 min On July 20 1969, only seven years later, an American became the first person ever to set foot on the moon His name was Neil Armstrong Millions of people watched on television as history was made As he took that first step onto the moon's surface he said That's one small step for a man, one giant leap for mankind. People all over the world heard and still remember those historic words.

Rewrite the story correctly on the lines below.

Brainwork! What important world events have happened in your lifetime? Make a list of three or more. Tell when and where each happened and why it was important. Proofread for periods and commas.

Name ______________________________ Skill: Proofreading, Spelling

Just Visiting

In the story below, some words sound right but have the wrong spelling for their meaning. Other words are misspelled because the spelling guidelines for making those words plural were forgotten. Read the story and circle the 12 misspelled words. (Hint: Five are the homonyms *there*, *their*, and *they're*. Seven are plurals for words that end in *y*, in *f*, or in *sh* or *ch*.)

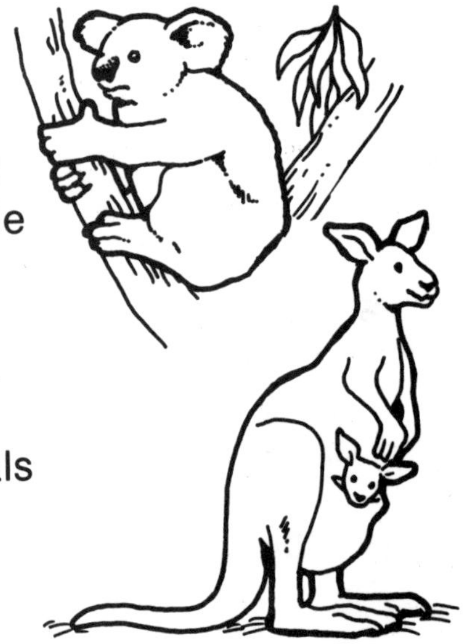

Just Visiting

They're are lots of different citys and countrys to see, but most of all I'd like to visit Australia. I've heard that the people their are friendly and the animals are most interesting. Kangaroos and koalas in the wild are only found they're. It would be great to see wild kangaroos hopping about with babys peeking out of there pouchs or koalas munching on eucalyptus leafs in the bushs. I think there the cutest animals in the world! To visit Australia is one of my greatest wishs.

Rewrite the story correctly on the lines below.

Brainwork! Write about the place you would most like to visit. Tell why you'd like to go there and what you could see and do. Proofread your story for spelling errors.

Answers

Page One
Capitalized: Our, Field, Trip, On, In, To, Fly, The, Next, I, What, It's, Like, Moon, Those, Flying, Machines

Page Two
Capitalized: August, Disney, Orlando, Florida, Thanksgiving, Savannah, Georgia, Savannah, Sunday, Wednesday, World

Page Three
Capitalized: Mr., Hunt, Dr., Barbara, Newley, Mrs., Lowe, Carmen, Miss, Compton, Dr., Newley, I

Page Four
Capitalized: Americans, Martin, Luther, King, Jr., Growing, Atlanta, Georgia, Martin, Believing, Dr., King, Though

Page Five
Capitalized: Days, Valentine's, Day, February, May, I, Mother's, Day, Collecting, My, Thoughts, August, Halloween, October, Friday, Saturday, New, Year's, Day, I

Page Six

Windy Weather

Once when I was two years old, the wind blew me over. How could something I couldn't see knock me down?

Wind is simply moving air. Sometimes the air seems almost still. Other times the wind is so strong it can push over a big tree!/. The force of the wind is measured in miles per hour (m.p.h.). At four to seven m.p.h. you may feel a slight breeze. At 32 m.p.h. it's hard to walk against the wind./! What do you think the speed of the wind was when it blew me over?

Page Seven

Dinosaur Days

Scientists have different ideas about how the dinosaurs looked. Some think they were big, green, scaly reptiles with small brains. Others think that some dinosaurs were warm-blooded, intelligent animals. Some dinosaurs were plant-eaters who dined on leaves, grass, and fruits. Others were meat-eaters who ate eggs, fish, birds, and other dinosaurs. Even though dinosaurs are long gone, scientists keep making new discoveries about these ancient, fascinating creatures.

Page Eight

My Myna Dinah

Someone came to my door. My myna Dinah said, "Hello!"

Many people think myna birds can talk, but they really only imitate sounds.

"How are you?" asked the visitor, and Dinah replied, "How are you?"

A myna's voice sounds surprisingly human. So the next time you think someone is talking to you, it could be Dinah—or some other myna!

Page Nine

News Flash!

On Nov. 30, 1987, the city spelling bee finally ended. Lee Hahn of 1412 Lyon Ave. accepted his first-place prize of one hundred dollars on Dec. 1, 1987. A ceremony was held at City Hall hosted by Mr. Alex Bate, U.S. senator from Missouri. Lee was one of eighty students who entered the contest on Sept. 9, 1987. His winning word was "leprechaun."

Page Ten

Night Visitor

It was a quiet, peaceful night. Suddenly I heard a whirring sound outside my window. I looked out to see that a spaceship had landed! It was silver, red, gold, and green. The door opened. Out walked an alien whose hair was fuzzy, purple, and strange. It had a round, red, and cute nose. "Is this the planet Zick?" he asked.

"No." I said.

"Sorry," he replied, "wrong planet." The door closed and the ship left as suddenly as it had come.

Page Eleven

Chester's Fur Flaps

In the winter of 1873 Chester Greenwood got ice skates for his fifteenth birthday. He ran to the pond **to** try them out, but couldn't stay **there** long—his ears were **too** cold! So Chester made **two** loops of wire covered with fur. Another wire fit over his head. Back **to** the pond he went. He couldn't hear **too** well, but his ears stayed warm! Chester's fur flaps became known as earmuffs and **they're** still keeping ears warm today.

Page Twelve
planning, creating, weddings, making, baking, popping, taking, coming, begging, tasting, smiling

Answers

Page Thirteen
elves, shelves, wishes, puppies, brushes, babies, elves

Page Fourteen

Best Friends

Today is not just any Wednesday—it's a special **Wednesday.** A year ago today, **February** 18, I met my best friend Katie. While I was in the **library,** it had started to snow. I didn't notice **because** I was busy reading. Later, Katie and I just happened to leave the library at the same time. We ended up walking home together in the snow. We exchanged phone numbers on a torn **piece** of paper. That snowy day was the beginning of our **friendship**.

Page Fifteen

Moving Day

It was **moving** day for Pete and his family. Mom was **taking** a terrific new job in **R**ichmond, **V**irginia. She told Pete that presidents Washington**,** Jefferson**,** and Madison were born there and that Pete would even be **living** on **M**onroe **S**treet! Pete packed his cap**,** mitt**,** baseball**,** and team shirt. He'd miss his friends in **G**rove **C**ity, **C**alifornia, but looked forward to **making** new friends and **having** new kinds of fun.

Page Sixteen
January 30**,** 1988
Dear Mr. Donald Sobol**,**
Your fan**,**

Page Seventeen

June 27**,** 1987

Dear **J**osé,
Did you know that I was born on **J**uly 4**,** 1976**?** That was America's 200th birthday**!**
Can you help us celebrate our birthday by coming to my party next **S**aturday at 6:00**?** Dan**, J**ill, Mark, and **T**ommy are invited, too. We'll have a cookout and play games. Then we'll all go to see fireworks. Will you let me know if you'll be there**?**

Your friend,
Glen

Page Eighteen
Capitalized: Jane, Chimps, Jane, Goodall, Born, London, England, Jane, Africa, She, Jane, They, Jane, My, Friends, Wild, Chimpanzees

Page Nineteen

Americans in Space

On Feb. 20**,** 1962, John Glenn, Jr. became the first American to orbit the earth. His flight lasted 4 hrs. 56 min. On July 20**,** 1969, only seven years later, an American became the first person ever to set foot on the moon**.** His name was Neil Armstrong**.** Millions of people watched on television as history was made**.** As he took that first step onto the moon's surface he said**,** "That's one small step for a man, one giant leap for mankind." People all over the world heard and still remember those historic words.

Page Twenty

Just Visiting

There are lots of different **cities** and **countries** to see, but most of all I'd like to visit Australia. I've heard that the people **there** are friendly and the animals are most interesting. Kangaroos and koalas in the wild are only found **there**. It would be great to see wild kangaroos hopping about with **babies** peeking out of **their** **pouches** or koalas munching on eucalyptus **leaves** in the **bushes**. I think **they're** the cutest animals in the world! To visit Australia is one of my greatest **wishes**